Umpire's *Adventure*
in Alphabet Town

by Laura Alden
illustrated by Linda Hohag

created by Wing Park Publishers

CP CHILDRENS PRESS ®
CHICAGO

Library of Congress Cataloging-in-Publication Data

Alden, Laura, 1955-
    Umpire's adventure in Alphabet Town / by Laura Alden ;
illustrated by Linda Hohag.
        p.   cm. — (Read around Alphabet Town)
    Summary: Ump wears his underwear while encountering "u"
words during a search for his lost uniform in Alphabet Town.
Includes alphabet activities.
   ISBN 0-516-05421-X
   [1. Alphabet.] I. Hohag, Linda, ill. II. Title. III. Series.
PZ7.A3586Um   1992
[E]—dc 20   92-12668
                                         CIP
                                         AC

Umpire's *Adventure*
in Alphabet Town

You are now entering Alphabet Town,
With houses from "A" to "Z."
I'm going on a "U" adventure today,
So come along with me.

This is the "U" house of Alphabet
Town. An umpire lives here. His
friends call him, "Ump."

Ump likes everything that begins
with the letter "u."

This is Ump's uniform. Ump loves his

uniform.

He wears it when he works.

Ump wears his uniform at home too.
He even wears it when he plays his

ukelele.

9

He wears it all the time— except
at bedtime.

Then Ump always wears long

underwear.

One night, Ump was very tired. He put on his underwear and climbed under the covers. Soon he fell asleep.

When Ump awoke, it was morning.
He reached for his uniform. But
it was gone.

"Uh-oh!" said Ump. He was very upset. He looked under the bed. He looked everywhere. No uniform!

"What will I wear?" he cried. "My
uniform is gone!"

Ump ran outside. He was so upset he forgot he was in his underwear!

Ump climbed on his

unicycle.

"I must find my uniform," he said.
And off he rode through Alphabet
Town.

Ump met an upside-down-cake baker.

"Have you seen my uniform?" he asked.

"No, but I hope you find it," said the upside-down-cake baker. "You look pretty silly in your underwear."

Next Ump met a

used-car salesman.

"Have you seen my uniform?"
Ump asked.

"I have not," said the used-car salesman. "But you look pretty silly in your underwear. Do you want to buy a used car?"

"No," said Ump, sadly. Just then it
started to sprinkle rain.

Ump got on his unicycle and started back to his "U" house.

On the way he bought an

umbrella

to keep his underwear dry.

Then Ump heard a truck coming. It was his uncle's laundry truck.

"Uncle," he shouted. "Do you have
my uniform?"
"Of course I do," said Ump's uncle.

"Today is wash day. I always take your uniform on wash day."
"Uh, sorry," said Ump. "I forgot."

"Well, put on your uniform," said his uncle. "You look pretty silly in your underwear." So Ump did just that.

Then Ump hurried home, and
he never forgot about wash
day again.

MORE FUN WITH UMP

What's in a Name?

In my "u" adventure, you read many "u" words. My name begins with a "U." Some of my friends' names begin with "U" too. Here are a few.

Una

Udele

Ursula

Udell

Upton

Ulysses

Do you know other names that start with "U"?

Does your name start with "U"?

Ump's Word Hunt

I like to hunt for "u" words. Can you help me find the words on this page that begin with "u"? How many are there? Can you read them?

usher

unicorn

bus

cat

truck

emu

under

Can you find any words with "u" in the middle?
Can you find any with "u" at the end?
Can you find a word with no "u"?

31

Ump's Favorite Things

"U" is my favorite letter. I love "u" things. Can you guess why? You can find some of my favorite "u" things in my house on page 7. How many "u" things can you find there? Can you think of more "u" things?

Now you make up a "u" adventure.